INTEGRATING Maps and Money with Reading Instruction

6 Complete Social Studies Units

Written by
Trisha Callella

Editor: LaDawn Walter
Illustrator: Jenny Campbell
Cover Illustrator: Rick Grayson
Designer/Production: Moonhee Pak/Mary Gagné
Cover Designer: Moonhee Pak
Art Director: Tom Cochrane
Project Director: Carolea Williams

Table of Contents

Introduction

For many students, reading comprehension diminishes when they read nonfiction text. Students often have difficulty understanding social studies vocabulary, making inferences, and grasping social studies concepts. With so much curriculum to cover each day, social studies content is sometimes put on the back burner when it comes to academic priorities. *Integrating Maps and Money with Reading Instruction* provides the perfect integration of social studies content with specific reading instruction to help students improve their comprehension of nonfiction text and maximize every minute of your teaching day.

This resource includes six units that tie in the themes of geography and economics. The units are based on the most common social studies topics taught in grades 3–4 in accordance with the national social studies standards:

City, County, State, and Country   **Latitude and Longitude**
National Geography   **Money and the Great Depression**
Finding Your Way with Maps   **Trading or Bartering**

Each unit includes powerful prereading strategies, such as predicting what the story will be about, accessing prior knowledge, and brainstorming about vocabulary that may be included in the reading selection. Following the prereading exercises is a nonfiction reading selection written on a grade 3–4 reading level. Each reading selection is followed by essential postreading activities such as comprehension questions on multiple taxonomy levels, skill reviews, and a critical thinking exercise. Each unit also includes a hands-on activity that connects each social studies topic to students' lives. The descriptions on pages 5–8 include the objectives and implementation strategies for each unit component.

Before, during, and after reading the story, students are exposed to the same reading strategies you typically reinforce during your language arts instruction block and guided reading. This powerful duo gives you the opportunity to teach both reading and social studies simultaneously. Using the activities in this resource, students will continue *learning to read* while *reading to learn*. They will become more successful readers while gaining new social studies knowledge and experiences.

Prereading Strategies

✓ Catch a Clue
✓ Concept Map
✓ Word Warm-Up

Nonfiction Text

Postreading Applications

✓ Comprehension Questions
✓ Sharpen Your Skills
✓ Get Logical

Hands-on Social Studies

Connections to Standards

This chart shows the concepts that are covered in each unit based on the national social studies standards.

	City, County, State, and Country	National Geography	Finding Your Way with Maps	Latitude and Longitude	Money and the Great Depression	Trading or Bartering
Compare and contrast differences about past events, people, places, or situations, and identify how they contribute to our understanding of the past.					●	●
Understand how scarcity and choice govern our economic decisions.					●	●
Distinguish between needs and wants.					●	●
Identify examples of private and public goods and services.						●
Describe the relationship of price to supply and demand.						●
Use economic concepts such as supply, demand, and price to help explain events in the community and nation.					●	
Locate and distinguish varying landforms and geographic features such as mountains, islands, and oceans.		●				
Use mental maps of locales, regions, and the world that demonstrate understanding of relative location, direction, size, and shape.	●	●	●	●		
Compare the information that can be derived from a three-dimensional model to that of a picture of the same location.			●	●		
Use resources such as atlases, grid systems, charts, graphs, and maps to generate, manipulate, and interpret information.			●	●		
Interpret, use, and distinguish various representations of the earth such as maps and globes.			●			
Distinguish between the North and South Poles, the equator and prime meridian, and the hemispheres using coordinates.				●		
Explain and use the coordinate grid system of latitude and longitude to determine the absolute locations of places on earth.				●		

Unit Overview

Catch a Clue

Objectives

Students will

✓ be introduced to key concepts and vocabulary *before* reading

✓ be able to transfer this key strategy to improve test-taking skills

Implementation

Students will use clues and the process of elimination to predict what the nonfiction reading selection will be about. Copy this page on an overhead transparency, and use it for a whole-class activity. Begin by reading aloud each word, and ask students to repeat the words. Read the clues one at a time. Then, discuss with the class what topic(s) could be eliminated and the reasons why. (Note: There will be clues that do not eliminate any topics. The purpose of this is to teach students that although there is information listed, it is not always helpful information.) Cross off a topic when the class decides that it does not fit the clues. If there is more than one topic left after the class discusses all of the clues, this becomes a prediction activity. When this occurs, reread the clues with the class, and discuss which answer would be most appropriate given the clues provided.

Concept Map

Objectives

Students will

✓ access prior knowledge by brainstorming what they already know about the topic

✓ increase familiarity with the social studies content by hearing others' prior knowledge experiences

✓ revisit the map *after* reading to recall information from the reading selection

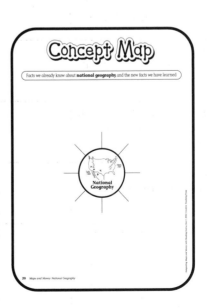

Implementation

Copy this page on an overhead transparency, and use it for a whole-class activity. Use a colored pen to write students' prior knowledge on the transparency. After the class reads the story, use a different colored pen to add what students learned.

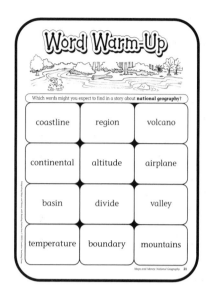

Word Warm-Up

Objectives

Students will

✓ be introduced to new vocabulary words

✓ make predictions about the story using thinking and reasoning skills

✓ begin to monitor their own comprehension

Implementation

Students will use the strategy of exclusion brainstorming to identify which words are likely to be in the story and which words are unrelated and should be eliminated from the list. Copy this page on an overhead transparency, and use it for a whole-class activity. Have students make predictions about which of the vocabulary words could be in the story and which words probably would not be in the story. Ask them to give reasons for their predictions. For example, say *Do you think airplanes would be in a story about geography?* A student may say *Yes, because airplanes are used to look at geography* or *No, because geography is not about transportation.* Circle the word if a student says that it will be in the story, and cross it out if a student says it will not be in the story. Do not correct students' responses. After reading, students can either confirm or disconfirm their own predictions. It is more powerful for students to verify their predictions on their own than to be told the answer before ever reading the story.

Nonfiction Text

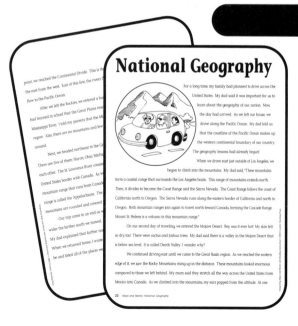

The Story

Objectives

Students will

✓ read high-interest, nonfiction stories

✓ increase social studies knowledge

✓ increase content area vocabulary

✓ make connections between social studies facts and their own experiences

Implementation

Give each student a copy of the story, and display the corresponding Word Warm-Up transparency while you read the story with the class. After the class reads the story, go back to the transparency, and have students discuss their predictions in relation to the new information they learned in the story. Invite students to identify any changes they would make on the transparency and give reasons for their responses. Then, revisit the corresponding Concept Map transparency, and write the new information students have learned.

Postreading Applications

Comprehension Questions

<u>Objectives</u>

Students will

✓ recall factual information

✓ be challenged to think beyond the story facts to make inferences

✓ connect the story to other reading, their own lives, and the world around them

<u>Implementation</u>

Use these questions to facilitate a class discussion of the story. Choose the number and types of questions that best meet the abilities of your class.

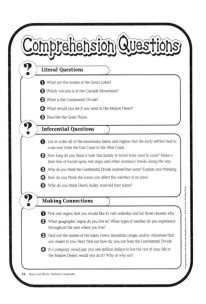

Sharpen Your Skills

<u>Objectives</u>

Students will

✓ practice answering questions in common test-taking formats

✓ integrate language arts skills with social studies knowledge

<u>Implementation</u>

After the class reads a story, give each student a copy of this page. Ask students to read each question and all of the answer choices for that question before deciding on an answer. Show them how to use their pencil to completely fill in the circle for their answer. Invite students to raise their hand if they have difficulty reading a question and/or the answer choices. Thoroughly explain the types of questions and exactly what is being asked the first few times students use this reproducible.

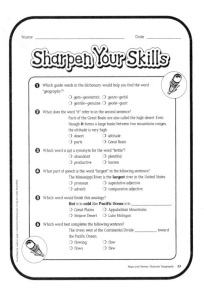

Get Logical

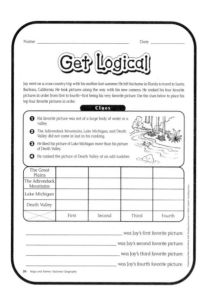

Objectives

Students will

✓ practice logical and strategic thinking skills

✓ practice the skill of process of elimination

✓ transfer the information read by applying it to new situations

Implementation

Give each student a copy of this page. Read the beginning sentences and the clues to familiarize students with the words. Show students step-by-step how to eliminate choices based on the clues given. Have students place an X in a box that represents an impossible choice, thereby narrowing down the options for accurate choices. Once students understand the concept, they can work independently on this reproducible.

Hands-on Social Studies

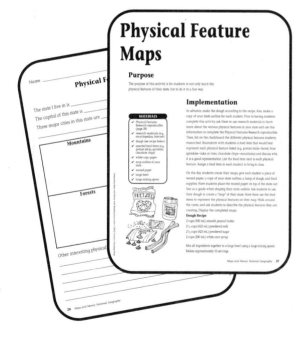

Social Studies Activity

Objectives

Students will

✓ participate in hands-on learning experiences

✓ expand and reinforce social studies knowledge

✓ apply new social studies vocabulary words

Implementation

The social studies activities in this book incorporate a variety of skills students are required to experience at this age level (e.g., survey, interview, analyze, evaluate). Each hands-on activity begins with an explanation of its purpose to help direct the intended learning. Give each student a copy of any corresponding reproducibles and/or materials for the activity. Then, introduce the activity and explain the directions. Model any directions that may be difficult for students to follow on their own.

Catch a Clue

Integrating Maps and Money with Reading Instruction © 2002 Creative Teaching Press

What will we learn about in our reading today?

ponds, rivers, and oceans

cities, counties, states, and countries

relatives and ancestors

senators and governors

Our Clues

1 We will not focus on bodies of water.

2 We will not focus on the past.

3 We will talk about where we live.

4 We will learn about government and geography.

Concept Map

Facts we already know about a **city, county, state, and country,** and the new facts we have learned

City, County, State, and Country

Word Warm-Up

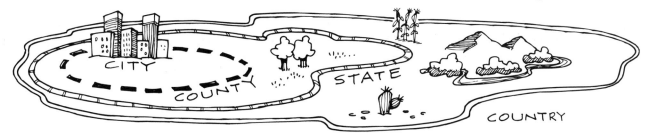

Which words might you expect to find in a story about a **city, county, state, and country?**

rocket	river	border
family	citizen	governor
democratic	mountain	paper
elects	continents	territory

City, County, State, and Country

Imagine you look out your front window one morning. In your front yard you see a rocket ship. You climb on board. As the rocket starts to rise, you see your house and yard as a bird might see it. You go higher. Then, you see how the street you live on is a part of a city. The rocket climbs even higher. Now, you can see nearby cities that are all a part of the county you live in. As the rocket climbs into the sky, your county joins with other counties. Now, you can see the area that makes up your state. Higher and higher the rocket climbs. The area that makes up your country is visible below. Soon, you are leaving the Earth. Below, you can see the outline of North America, the continent you live on. As the rocket travels into space, you see the continents and oceans that make up the planet you live on, Earth.

City, county, state, and country. Each of these places is a part of something larger. You have a place in all four of these areas. However, these areas are hard to see. The border of each could be a river or even a mountain range. Most of the time, the border cannot be seen. Only a map would show where the borders lie.

What is a city? A city is a group of people living and working together. A city can be a few people or it can be a million people. A city has its own government. A mayor is the leader of the city. The government decides how to serve the people who live there. It provides the police, the firefighters, and other services that help people.

What is a county? A county is an area within a state that may include many cities or towns.

Integrating Maps and Money with Reading Instruction © 2002 Creative Teaching Press

It is a way for the state to better manage an area and divide its resources. For example, all of the cities in a county may share the cost of building and maintaining the roads. Each county decides how it wants to run things. The people in the county decide what is best for their area.

What is a state? A state is a territory within a country. For example, Texas is a state in the United States. Each state has its own government. Each state elects a governor to act as its leader. A state decides which laws are best for its people. The government of a state takes care of the people, the land, and the natural resources found inside its borders.

What is a country? A country is a nation that is separate from other nations. For example, fifty states are joined together to form the United States. This country has borders that separate it from other countries. The country of Mexico is to the south of it. The country of Canada is to the north of it. The Pacific Ocean borders it on the west. To the east, the border is the Atlantic Ocean.

A country has its own government and leaders. There are many countries all around the world. Each country has a different type of government. In the United States, there is a democratic government. This means that the people elect who will act as their leaders. They elect a president to lead and represent their country. The citizens elect other people to represent each state.

The country of the United States is divided up into separate states. Each state is divided into counties. Each county is made up of many cities. Each city is made up of businesses, homes, streets, parks, and schools. What do these all have in common? You are a citizen of each of these places.

Comprehension Questions

1. What is a city?

2. What is a county?

3. What is a state?

4. What is a country?

5. What type of government does the United States have? What does it mean to have this type of government?

 Inferential Questions

1. Why is the United States divided up into states? What problems could there be if the United States was just one gigantic state?

2. Why do you think different countries carefully watch people who cross the borders into their land?

3. Why do you think states have borders if you are able to freely cross them?

4. Why is the president important to the United States?

5. How is your school like a country? What part of the school would be like states? What part of the school would be like cities? Who governs your school?

 Making Connections

1. What city, county, state, and country do you live in?

2. Who are the people in charge of your city, county, state, and country?

3. Look at a map of your city, a map of your state, and a map of your country. Create a three-circle Venn diagram to show how they are all similar and how they are all unique.

4. If you were to run for a government office, would you choose to be a part of a city, county, state, or country government? Why?

Integrating Maps and Money with Reading Instruction © 2002 Creative Teaching Press

Sharpen Your Skills

1 Which guide words in the dictionary would help you find the word "state"?

- ○ skirt–slack   ○ soap–social
- ○ stall–standard   ○ start–status

2 Which word is <u>not</u> a synonym for the word "certain" in the following sentence?

One part of a state may have **certain** things it wants or needs.

- ○ particular   ○ vague
- ○ specific   ○ distinct

3 How would you split the word "government" into syllables?

- ○ gov-er-n-ment   ○ go-vern-ment
- ○ gov-ern-ment   ○ go-ver-n-ment

4 What part of speech is the word "democratic" in the following sentence?

In the United States, there is a **democratic** government.

- ○ adjective   ○ verb
- ○ adverb   ○ noun

5 Which word would finish this analogy?

Philadelphia is to **city** like _____ is to **state.**

- ○ Missouri   ○ United States
- ○ New York City   ○ Orange County

6 Which word best completes the following sentence?

The city elected _____ new officials.

- ○ their   ○ they're
- ○ there   ○ theer

Name _____   Date _____

Get Logical

There were four guest speakers at the charity event. Each speaker was an elected official or was running for office. Each person spoke about his or her job and area. Use the clues below to decide who works in each area of government.

Clues

1. Ms. Penner does not govern a state.

2. Mr. Olson does not govern a city or county. He was running for an office that has a term of four years.

3. Mr. Kominsky works for the city. He is not the mayor.

4. Ms. Consuelos is in charge of a state.

	Mr. Kominsky	Ms. Penner	Ms. Consuelos	Mr. Olson
Mayor				
Governor				
Manager				
President				

Mr. Kominsky is the _____.

Ms. Penner is the _____.

Ms. Consuelos is the _____.

Mr. Olson is the _____.

Integrating Maps and Money with Reading Instruction © 2002 Creative Teaching Press

City, County, State, and Country Flip Book

Purpose

The purpose of this activity is for students to gain an understanding of the difference between their own city, county, state, and country and to learn interesting facts about each one.

MATERIALS

✔ City, County, State, and Country Research reproducible (page 18)

✔ scissors

✔ blue, green, orange, and yellow construction paper

✔ stapler

✔ research materials (e.g., books, encyclopedias)

✔ crayons or markers

✔ copies of outlines of your city, county, state, and country (optional)

Implementation

In advance, make a flip book for each student. For each student, cut a 4$1/2$" x 12" (11.5 cm x 30.5 cm) piece of blue construction paper, a 4$1/2$" x 10" (11.5 cm x 25.5 cm) piece of green construction paper, a 4$1/2$" x 8" (11.5 cm x 20 cm) piece of orange construction paper, and a 4$1/2$" x 6" (11.5 cm x 15 cm) piece of yellow construction paper. Stack the papers in order of size from largest to smallest. Align the tops of the papers, and staple them together across the top. Give each student a City, County, State, and Country Research reproducible. Invite students to use research materials to complete their reproducible. Then, give each student a flip book. Have students label the bottom left-hand corner of their four pages as follows: *City, County, State,* and *Country*. Then, ask students to write the name of each of these places according to where they live on the corresponding right-hand corner flap. Invite students to draw an outline of or a symbol that represents each of these places on the corresponding flap, color their drawings, and write some facts about each place. For example, students living in the state of Iowa would draw an outline of that state and write some interesting facts they have learned about Iowa. Another option is to have students color and cut out a copy of a state outline and/or a symbol that represents each place.

City, County, State, and Country Research

I.   Name of my city: _____

   A. Three interesting facts:

   1. _____

   2. _____

   3. _____

II.   Name of my county: _____

   A. Three interesting facts:

   1. _____

   2. _____

   3. _____

III.   Name of my state: _____

   A. Three interesting facts:

   1. _____

   2. _____

   3. _____

IV.   Name of my country: _____

   A. Three interesting facts:

   1. _____

   2. _____

   3. _____

Integrating Maps and Money with Reading Instruction © 2002 Creative Teaching Press

Catch a Clue

Integrating Maps and Money with Reading Instruction © 2002 Creative Teaching Press

What will we learn about in our reading today?

national geography

Gold Rush

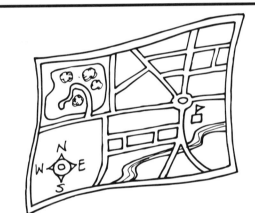

how to use maps

early pioneers

Our Clues

1 We will talk about California.

2 It involves some traveling.

3 We will discuss places across the country.

4 We will learn about regions, mountain ranges, and the Great Lakes.

Concept Map

Facts we already know about **national geography,** and the new facts we have learned

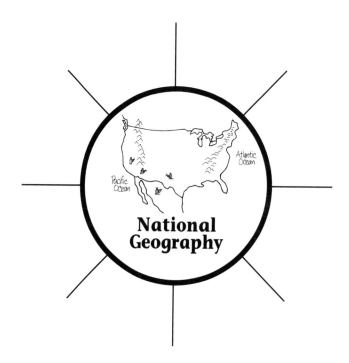

National Geography

Integrating Maps and Money with Reading Instruction © 2002 Creative Teaching Press

Word Warm-Up

Which words might you expect to find in a story about **national geography?**

coastline	region	volcano
continental	altitude	airplane
basin	divide	valley
temperature	boundary	mountains

National Geography

For a long time, my family had planned to drive across the United States. My dad said it was important for us to learn about the geography of our nation. Now, the day had arrived. As we left our house, we drove along the Pacific Ocean. My dad told us that the coastline of the Pacific Ocean makes up the western continental boundary of our country. The geography lessons had already begun!

When we drove east just outside of Los Angeles, we began to climb into the mountains. My dad said, "These mountains form a coastal range that surrounds the Los Angeles basin. This range of mountains extends north. Then, it divides to become the Coast Range and the Sierra Nevada. The Coast Range follows the coast of California north to Oregon. The Sierra Nevada runs along the eastern border of California and north to Oregon. Both mountain ranges join again to travel north toward Canada, forming the Cascade Range. Mount St. Helens is a volcano in this mountain range."

On our second day of traveling, we entered the Mojave Desert. Boy, was it ever hot! My skin felt so dry, too! There were cactus and Joshua trees. My dad said there is a valley in the Mojave Desert that is below sea level. It is called Death Valley. I wonder why?

We continued driving east until we came to the Great Basin region. As we reached the eastern edge of it, we saw the Rocky Mountains rising up in the distance. These mountains looked enormous compared to those we left behind. My mom said they stretch all the way across the United States from Mexico into Canada. As we climbed into the mountains, my ears popped from the altitude. At one

Integrating Maps and Money with Reading Instruction © 2002 Creative Teaching Press

point, we reached the Continental Divide. This is the line along the Rocky Mountain Range that divides the east from the west. East of this line, the rivers flow to the Atlantic Ocean. West of this line, the rivers flow to the Pacific Ocean.

After we left the Rockies, we entered a huge span of level grassland. It was the Great Plains. I had learned in school that the Great Plains reach from the base of the Rocky Mountains to the Mississippi River. I told my parents that the Missouri and Mississippi Rivers drain the Great Plains region. Also, there are no mountains and few hills. It was true. All we saw was flat land for miles around.

Next, we headed northeast to the Great Lakes. These lakes are the largest in the United States. There are five of them: Huron, Ohio, Michigan, Erie, and Superior. The Great Lakes are connected to each other. The St. Lawrence River connects them to the Atlantic Ocean. The lakes form part of the United States border with Canada. As we headed southeast from the Great Lakes, we crossed a mountain range that runs from Canada all the way down to Alabama. The southern part of this range is called the Appalachians. The Adirondack Mountains stretch north of New York. These mountains are rounded and covered with forests.

Our trip came to an end as we traveled into the eastern coastal region. This coastal region got wider the farther south we moved. Many rivers, islands, bays, and inlets were located along the shore. My dad explained that farther north into New England, the coast is rugged, rocky, and at times cold. When we returned home, I wrote in my journal about how different the regions in the United States can be and listed all of the places we visited. This country of ours is quite a special place!

Comprehension Questions

Literal Questions

1. What are the names of the Great Lakes?

2. Which volcano is in the Cascade Mountains?

3. What is the Continental Divide?

4. What would you see if you went to the Mojave Desert?

5. Describe the Great Plains.

Inferential Questions

1. List in order all of the mountains, lakes, and regions that the early settlers had to cross over from the East Coast to the West Coast.

2. How long do you think it took this family to travel from coast to coast? Make a time line of tourist spots, rest stops, and other necessary breaks along the way.

3. Why do you think the Continental Divide received that name? Explain your thinking.

4. How do you think the ocean can affect the weather of an area?

5. Why do you think Death Valley received that name?

Making Connections

1. Pick one region that you would like to visit someday and list three reasons why.

2. What geographic region do you live in? What types of weather do you experience throughout the year where you live?

3. Find out the names of the lakes, rivers, mountain ranges, and/or volcanoes that are closest to you. Next, find out how far you are from the Continental Divide.

4. If a company would pay you one million dollars to live the rest of your life in the Mojave Desert, would you do it? Why or why not?

Integrating Maps and Money with Reading Instruction © 2002 Creative Teaching Press

Sharpen Your Skills

1 Which guide words in the dictionary would help you find the word "geography"?

    ○ gem–geocentric   ○ genre–gerbil
    ○ gentile–genuine   ○ geode–giant

2 What does the word "it" refer to in the second sentence?

    Parts of the Great Basin are also called the high desert. Even though **it** forms a large basin between two mountains ranges, the altitude is very high.

    ○ desert   ○ altitude
    ○ parts   ○ Great Basin

3 Which word is <u>not</u> a synonym for the word "fertile"?

    ○ abundant   ○ plentiful
    ○ productive   ○ barren

4 What part of speech is the word "largest" in the following sentence?

    The Mississippi River is the **largest** river in the United States.

    ○ pronoun   ○ superlative adjective
    ○ adverb   ○ comparative adjective

5 Which word would finish this analogy?

    Hot is to **cold** like **Pacific Ocean** is to _____.

    ○ Great Plains   ○ Appalachian Mountains
    ○ Mojave Desert   ○ Lake Michigan

6 Which word best completes the following sentence?

    The rivers west of the Continental Divide _____ toward the Pacific Ocean.

    ○ flowing   ○ flow
    ○ flows   ○ flew

Get Logical

Jay went on a cross-country trip with his mother last summer. He left his home in Florida to travel to Santa Barbara, California. He took pictures along the way with his new camera. He ranked his four favorite pictures in order from first to fourth—first being his very favorite picture. Use the clues below to place his top four favorite pictures in order.

Clues

1 His favorite picture was not of a large body of water or a valley.

2 The Adirondack Mountains, Lake Michigan, and Death Valley did not come in last in his ranking.

3 He liked his picture of Lake Michigan more than his picture of Death Valley.

4 He ranked the picture of Death Valley at an odd number.

	First	Second	Third	Fourth
The Great Plains				
The Adirondack Mountains				
Lake Michigan				
Death Valley				

_____ was Jay's first favorite picture.

_____ was Jay's second favorite picture.

_____ was Jay's third favorite picture.

_____ was Jay's fourth favorite picture.

Integrating Maps and Money with Reading Instruction © 2002 Creative Teaching Press

Physical Feature Maps

Purpose

The purpose of this activity is for students to not only learn the physical features of their state, but to do it in a fun way.

Implementation

In advance, make the dough according to the recipe. Also, make a copy of your state outline for each student. Prior to having students complete this activity, ask them to use research materials to learn more about the various physical features in your state and use this information to complete the Physical Features Research reproducible. Then, list on the chalkboard the different physical features students researched. Brainstorm with students a food item that would best represent each physical feature listed (e.g., pretzel sticks—forest, blue sprinkles—lake or river, chocolate chips—mountains) and discuss why it is a good representation. List the food item next to each physical feature. Assign a food item to each student to bring to class.

On the day students create their maps, give each student a piece of waxed paper, a copy of your state outline, a lump of dough, and food supplies. Have students place the waxed paper on top of the state out-line as a guide when shaping their state outline. Ask students to use their dough to create a "map" of their state. Have them use the food items to represent the physical features on their map. Walk around the room, and ask students to describe the physical features they are creating. Display the completed maps.

Dough Recipe

2 cups (500 mL) smooth peanut butter

$2\frac{1}{2}$ cups (625 mL) powdered milk

$2\frac{1}{2}$ cups (625 mL) powdered sugar

2 cups (500 mL) white corn syrup

Mix all ingredients together in a large bowl using a large mixing spoon. Makes approximately 10 servings.

Name _____   Date _____

Physical Features Research

The state I live in is _____.

The capital of this state is _____.

Three major cities in this state are _____

_____.

Mountains	**Lakes, Rivers, Oceans**
Forests	**Deserts**

Other interesting physical features are _____

_____

_____

_____

_____

_____

Catch a Clue

What will we learn about in our reading today?

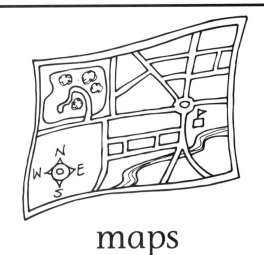

maps

state governments

missions

banks

Our Clues

1 They are important in your life.

2 Your family uses them.

3 They are flat.

4 They help you find where you are going.

Concept Map

Facts we already know about **maps,** and the new facts we have learned

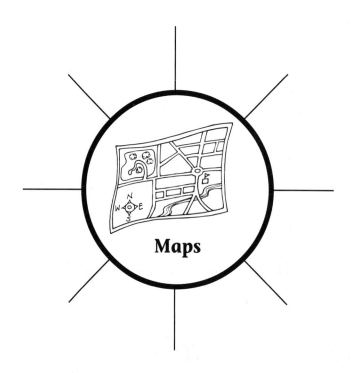

Maps

Word Warm-Up

Mobility Map

General Reference Map

Which words might you expect to find in a story about **maps?**

inventory	sphere	orange
mobility	alphabetical	imaginary
coordinate	symbol	features
pilots	continents	dictionary

Finding Your Way with Maps

A globe is a model of the earth. It is the same shape as the earth, but it is a different size. A globe shows us the location of the continents, oceans, deserts, and mountain ranges. Often, it shows the locations of different countries. A globe is the best representation of our world, but flat maps are cheaper and easier to use. A map is a flat symbol of our world. The first maps helped people get from one place to another. A map could be rolled or folded and put away. Imagine Christopher Columbus on the deck of his ship trying to find his way with a globe in his hands! Today, there are four different types of maps that fit different purposes. They are reference maps, inventory maps, thematic maps, and mobility maps.

General reference maps are the most familiar kind of map. These maps help you find and identify features of the land. Lakes, rivers, mountains, islands, and other physical features are on a general reference map. These maps may also show the borders of cities, counties, states, or other cultural features.

Inventory maps show exactly where a specific place is located. An inventory map might show where all of the dairy farms are located in your state. It might show the locations of our nation's national parks. An inventory map allows you to count the number of locations of a specific type of place.

Thematic maps show the amounts of different things. A thematic map often uses different

Integrating Maps and Money with Reading Instruction © 2002 Creative Teaching Press

colors as symbols. For example, a thematic map might show the amount of rainfall that falls in different parts of your state. The map might show areas where there is over 50 inches (127 cm) of rainfall a year in red. It may show areas where there is less than 20 inches (51 cm) of rainfall a year in blue.

Mobility maps help people get from one place to another. These are the types of maps your family uses for travel. Mobility maps include highway maps, street maps, and transit maps. Pilots and boat captains use mobility maps that are called charts.

To read a map, you need to know the "language." A compass rose is a symbol on the map that tells direction. The compass rose shows north, south, east, and west. The map key, or legend, explains what each symbol stands for on the map. The map scale shows how the distance on a map relates to the distance in real life. For example, 1 inch (2.5 cm) on a map might be equal to 1 mile (1.6 km) in real life. A map index helps you locate places on a map. It lists points of interest and where they can be found on the map.

A map is divided into a geographic grid. This grid is a set of imaginary lines that cross. One set of lines runs across the map in rows. Each row is labeled with a letter. The other set of lines runs in columns from top to bottom. Each column is labeled with a number. Sometimes the letters will label the columns and the numbers label the rows. Either way, each location on a map is given a coordinate. A coordinate contains a letter and a number. To find a location, use your finger to follow the letter and number to the place they meet on the page. In this square, you will find your location. Now you will never be lost using maps!

Comprehension Questions

1. What are the four main types of maps?
2. What can a general reference map help you find?
3. Describe a thematic map.
4. What is an inventory map?
5. Explain how to use a geographic grid.

 Inferential Questions

1. If 1 inch on a map were equal to $1\frac{1}{2}$ miles in real life, how many miles would 3 inches represent?

2. If 2 centimeters on a map were equal to 3 kilometers, how many kilometers would 5 centimeters represent?

3. Compare and contrast inventory maps and general reference maps.

4. When would a globe be more helpful than a map? When would a map be more helpful than a globe?

5. Why do you think so many different kinds of maps are necessary?

 Making Connections

1. Collect as many maps as you can. Label each type of map with one of the types of maps you read about (i.e., general reference, inventory, mobility, and thematic).

2. Look at a map of your city. Find where you live. What are the coordinates for your home? The local grocery store? Your school?

3. Look at a map of your city. Find where you live and where your school is located. Tell a friend which directions you need to travel to and from school.

4. Have you ever read a map at an amusement park? What symbols were used in the legend?

Integrating Maps and Money with Reading Instruction © 2002 Creative Teaching Press

Sharpen Your Skills

1 Which guide words in the dictionary would help you find the word "cartographer"?

○ conduct–cut   ○ cardiogram–carpal

○ cast–cataract   ○ carnivore–carve

2 What kind of sentence is the following sentence?

Do you know the difference between inventory and mobility maps?

○ exclamatory   ○ declarative

○ interrogative   ○ command

3 If you wanted to find an antonym for the word "locate," which resource would be the most helpful?

○ encyclopedia   ○ dictionary

○ thesaurus   ○ almanac

4 Which word is an adverb in the following sentence?

Would you be able to quickly find your street on a map of your city?

○ would   ○ map

○ quickly   ○ find

5 Which word would finish this analogy?

Compass is to _____ like **legend** is to **symbol.**

○ pictures   ○ inventories

○ directions   ○ distances

6 Which words best complete the following sentence?

You can find the coordinates of major _____ on the maps in any world atlas.

○ city and country   ○ citys and countrys

○ cities and countries ○ city and countries

Get Logical

The Best Bargain Bookstore is having its semiannual map blowout sale! There are four different tables displaying each type of map. The tables have a red, blue, green, or yellow tablecloth on them to get the shoppers' attention. Use the clues below to decide which type of map is on each color-coded table.

Clues

1 The rainfall maps are not on the yellow or blue table.

2 The maps identifying features such as mountains and islands are not on the blue or green table.

3 The maps showing how many dairy farms are located in a state are not on the blue, green, or yellow table.

4 The maps used by pilots and boat captains are on the blue table.

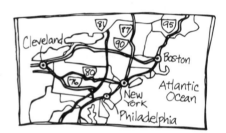

	Red	Blue	Green	Yellow
Mobility Maps				
Thematic Maps				
General Reference Maps				
Inventory Maps				

The red table is displaying the _____.

The blue table is displaying the _____.

The green table is displaying the _____.

The yellow table is displaying the _____.

Integrating Maps and Money with Reading Instruction © 2002 Creative Teaching Press

Space Rocket Grid

Purpose

The purpose of this activity is for students to practice using grid coordinates to become more familiar with how to use grid coordinates to locate points on a map.

Implementation

Discuss with students the concept of coordinates on a map. Review the information from the story: a coordinate is the meeting point of a given letter and number and pinpoints a location. In the same way, students will use coordinates to create a picture of a space rocket. Give each student a Space Rocket Coordinates reproducible and a Coordinate Grid. Explain that students must complete the coordinates in order to accurately draw the picture. For each space rocket coordinate, students find the letter on the left-hand side of their grid, find the number at the bottom of the page, and follow those lines until they meet. That is the coordinate point. Ask students to mark a dot with their pencil at that point. After students complete a set of coordinate points, invite them to connect the dots. Then, have them repeat the steps above for the remaining sets of coordinate points. Invite students to color their completed picture. As an extension, bring in actual maps, and invite students to use this same skill to find locations on the maps. Explain that on a map the coordinates locate a box rather than a point on a grid. Remind students that maps vary as to whether the letters or numbers run along the top or side of the map, but that they still find the coordinate point in the same way.

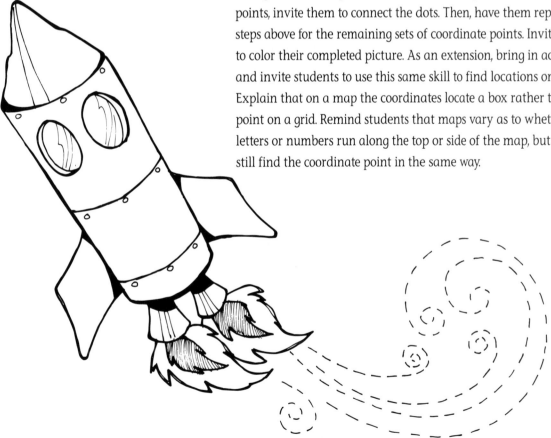

Space Rocket Coordinates

Set #1

(G, 1) (F, 2) (G, 3) (G, 4) (G, 5) (G, 6) (G, 7) (G, 8) (G, 9) (F, 10) (E, 11)

(D, 10) (C, 9) (C, 8) (C, 7) (C, 6) (C, 5) (C, 4) (C, 3) (D, 2) (C, 1) (G, 1)

Set #2

(G, 3) (H, 2) (I, 4) (H, 5) (G, 6) (G, 3)

Set #3

(C, 3) (B, 2) (A, 4) (B, 5) (C, 6) (C, 3)

Set #4

(F, 2) (D, 2)

Set #5

(E, 2) (E, 1)

Set #6

(F, 4) (F, 5) (D, 5) (D, 4) (F, 4)

Set #7

(F, 6) (F, 7) (D, 7) (D, 6) (F, 6)

Set #8

(F, 8) (F, 9) (D, 9) (D, 8) (F, 8)

Set #9

(G, 5) (H, 4) (G, 4) (H, 3)

Set #10

(C, 5) (B, 4) (C, 4) (B, 3)

Set #11

(F, 1) (G, 0)

Set #12

(F, 1) (F, 0)

Set #13

(F, 1) (E, 0)

Set #14

(D, 1) (E, 0)

Set #15

(D, 1) (D, 0)

Set #16

(D, 1) (C, 0)

Integrating Maps and Money with Reading Instruction © 2002 Creative Teaching Press

Name _____   Date _____

Coordinate Grid

	0	1	2	3	4	5	6	7	8	9	10	11	12
A													
B													
C													
D													
E													
F													
G													
H													
I													

Integrating Maps and Money with Reading Instruction © 2002 Creative Teaching Press

Catch a Clue

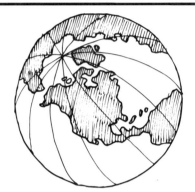

latitude and longitude

legends

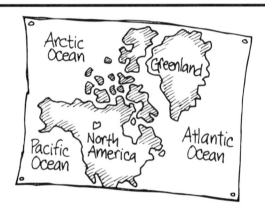

continents and oceans

streets and cities

Our Clues

❶ We will be studying geography.

❷ We will look carefully at the globe.

❸ We will talk about the North Pole and South Pole.

❹ We will pinpoint exact locations using lines of degree.

Integrating Maps and Money with Reading Instruction © 2002 Creative Teaching Press

Concept Map

Facts we already know about **latitude and longitude,** and the new facts we have learned

Latitude and Longitude

Word Warm-Up

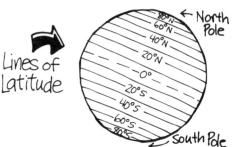

Lines of Latitude

Lines of Longitude

Which words might you expect to find in a story about **latitude and longitude?**

horizon	explore	equator
parallel	Columbus	hemisphere
measuring	finger	globe
degrees	prime meridian	expensive

Integrating Maps and Money with Reading Instruction © 2002 Creative Teaching Press

Latitude and Longitude

Hundreds of years ago, people did not like to sail very far out to sea. They thought that the world was flat. They thought ships would sail off the edge of the Earth. Even after people knew the Earth was round, ships followed the coastline. This way they could tell where they were by the landmarks on the shore. Soon, people wanted to explore far into the oceans. They needed a way to be able to tell where they were. Because of this, the idea of latitude and longitude was developed. By using latitude and longitude, a person can tell where he or she is on the planet Earth at any location.

If we want to tell someone where we are on the planet, we need to start measuring from the same place. Let's start with the North Pole and the South Pole. The poles are at opposite ends of the Earth. They are an equal distance apart. Halfway between the two poles is the widest part of the Earth. There is an imaginary line at this halfway point. It is called the equator. The equator divides the planet into two equal halves. The bottom half is called the Southern Hemisphere. The top half is called the Northern Hemisphere.

Lines of latitude are parallel to each other and the equator. They circle the planet. They divide it into sections. The circles get smaller as they get closer to the poles. Sometimes they are called parallels. Lines of latitude are labeled by degrees. The equator is at 0 degrees. The poles are both at 90 degrees. Any line of latitude in the Northern Hemisphere is a number of degrees north.

Any line of latitude in the Southern Hemisphere is a number of degrees south. That is how we can tell if we are moving toward the North Pole or the South Pole.

Knowing just the latitude does not help us find an exact location. If we say we are at zero degrees latitude, we know we are on the equator. But, we could be anywhere on the equator. That is a lot of distance! We only know where we are compared to the North or South Pole.

Lines of longitude run from the North Pole and meet again at the South Pole. They cross lines of latitude to help us find the exact location of a place. Think of the Earth as a giant orange. The line between each segment of the orange is like a line of longitude. Notice how the lines meet at one end. They get farther apart toward the middle of the orange. The lines meet again at the other end. At the equator, they are farthest apart.

Lines of latitude start with the equator, but where do lines of longitude start? They start with the prime meridian. This is an imaginary line that runs through Greenwich, England. This is the starting point because this is where the idea of longitude began. We measure the prime meridian at 0 degrees longitude. The degrees of longitude are measured from 0 to 180 degrees. If we cut the planet in half along the prime meridian, we would divide the planet into the Eastern and Western Hemispheres. If we move toward the west, we are moving in degrees longitude west. We would be in the Western Hemisphere. If we move toward the east, we are moving in degrees longitude east. We would be in the Eastern Hemisphere.

Now we can find any spot on planet Earth. The location of any spot is where the lines of latitude and longitude cross each other. For example, Columbus, Ohio, is at 40 degrees latitude north and 83 degrees longitude west. Can you find that city on a globe? What is the exact location of your city?

Integrating Maps and Money with Reading Instruction © 2002 Creative Teaching Press

Comprehension Questions

Integrating Maps and Money with Reading Instruction © 2002 Creative Teaching Press

Literal Questions

❶ In which directions do the lines of latitude run? Where is zero degrees latitude?

❷ In which directions do the lines of longitude run? Where are they farthest apart?

❸ What is the top half of the world above the equator called?

❹ What is the bottom half of the world below the equator called?

❺ What is the half of the world to the west of the prime meridian called? What is the half of the world to the east of the prime meridian called?

Inferential Questions

❶ Why are the lines of latitude and longitude helpful to ship captains and airline pilots? What do you think would happen if captains and pilots did not have them to use?

❷ Why do you think degrees are used to determine latitude and longitude?

❸ Why do the longitude lines get closer together at the poles?

❹ How many degrees go all the way around the Earth?

❺ What are the exact coordinates for the North Pole, the South Pole, and where the prime meridian crosses the equator?

Making Connections

❶ Where do you live? Find the location on a globe. What are your closest lines of latitude and longitude?

❷ Research three other jobs that involve the use of lines of latitude and longitude. Explain why they are important for each job.

❸ List the cities where each of your family members are from. Use a globe to find the lines of latitude and longitude for each city, and add this information to your page.

❹ Think of a place in the world you would like to visit someday. What are the lines of latitude and longitude of that place?

Sharpen Your Skills

1 How would you split the word "longitude" into syllables?
- ○ lon-gi-tude
- ○ long-i-tude
- ○ lo-ngi-tude
- ○ lon-git-ude

2 Which sentence below states an opinion—not a fact?
- ○ The lines of latitude run east and west.
- ○ The lines of longitude run north and south.
- ○ The lines of longitude are more important to sailors than latitude.
- ○ The lines of latitude begin at the equator.

3 Which word is the singular form of the word "halves" in the following sentence?

The equator divides the planet into two equal **halves.**
- ○ have
- ○ halfes
- ○ half
- ○ has

4 Which word is a synonym for the word "segment" in the following sentence?

Think of the Earth as a giant orange. The line between each **segment** of the orange is like a line of longitude.
- ○ line
- ○ whole
- ○ seed
- ○ section

5 Which word would finish this analogy?

Latitude is to **equator** like **longitude** is to _____.
- ○ Earth
- ○ degrees
- ○ South Pole
- ○ prime meridian

6 Which word best completes the following sentence?

The lines of latitude and longitude _____ people in finding exact locations on globes and maps.
- ○ ade
- ○ aid
- ○ aide
- ○ eight

Integrating Maps and Money with Reading Instruction © 2002 Creative Teaching Press

Get Logical

Tom and his friends made up a game to practice finding locations using latitude and longitude. One person spins the globe and another person stops the globe with one finger. The next person has to say the coordinates of that location. Tom is playing with his friends Brenton, Francie, Chloe, and Cristina. Use the clues below to decide which location each friend's finger ends up at on the globe at the end of the game.

Clues

1 Francie began at the prime meridian but ended up west of it.

2 The person whose finger ended up exactly in the middle of the North and South Poles was not Chloe.

3 The person whose finger ended up at Greenwich, England, was not Cristina.

4 Chloe ended up far south of the equator.

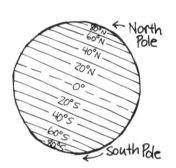

	Brenton	Francie	Chloe	Cristina
South Pole				
Western Hemisphere				
Equator				
Prime Meridian				

Brenton ended up on the _____.

Francie ended up on the _____.

Chloe ended up on the _____.

Cristina ended up on the _____.

The Great Globe Game

Purpose

The purpose of this activity is for students to practice recognizing, locating, and following the lines of latitude and longitude.

MATERIALS

- ✔ Direction Game Spinners (page 49)
- ✔ Number Game Spinners (page 50)
- ✔ Great Globe Locations reproducible (page 51)
- ✔ paper or card stock
- ✔ scissors
- ✔ brass fasteners
- ✔ paper clips
- ✔ globes

Implementation

For each small group of students, copy the Direction Game Spinners and a Number Game Spinner on paper or card stock. Cut out each spinner. Use a brass fastener to attach a paper clip to the center of each spinner. Divide the class into groups of four or five students. Give each student a Great Globe Locations reproducible. Give each group a set of spinners (i.e., north/south, east/west, and number) and a globe. Explain the rules of the game, and review your expectations, including good sportsmanship and quiet voices. Model how to play, record scores, and find a location on the globe, if necessary. Have students play for 15–20 minutes. Then, ask students to count how many different continents they visited. The player in each group that visited the most continents wins the game.

Game Rules

1. For each turn, start at the point where the equator crosses the prime meridian.
2. Spin the number spinner and the north/south spinner.
3. Write on your Great Globe Locations paper the number and direction that you landed on (e.g., 40 north).
4. Spin the number spinner again and the east/west spinner.
5. Write on your paper the number and direction that you landed on (e.g., 10 west).
6. Find the place where the two directions meet on the globe and name the location (e.g., 40 north, 10 west is closest to Portugal).
7. Record the name of the location in the third column of your paper.
8. The next player repeats steps 1–7 for his or her turn.

Integrating Maps and Money with Reading Instruction © 2002 Creative Teaching Press

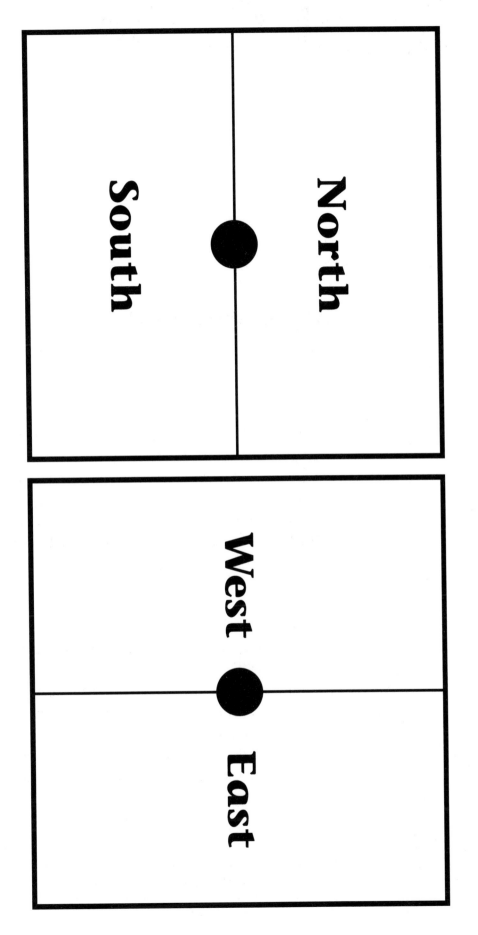

Number Game Spinners

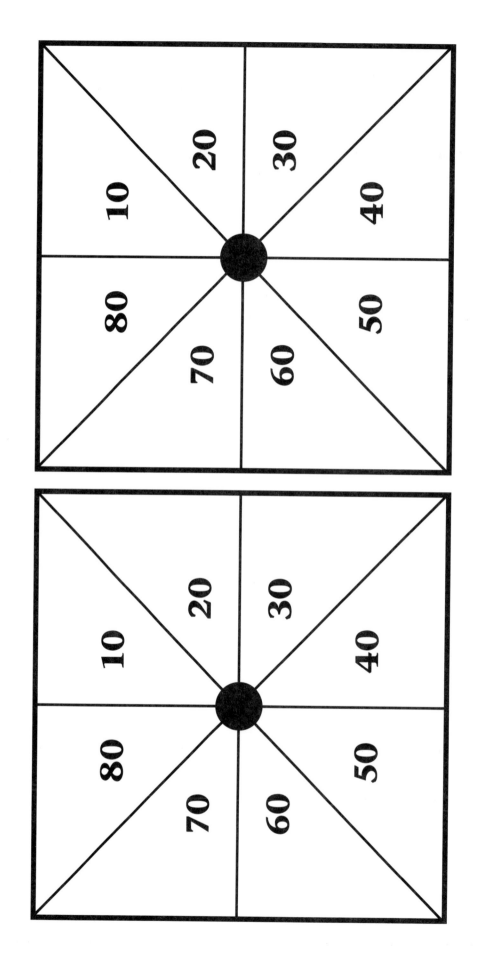

Integrating Maps and Money with Reading Instruction © 2002 Creative Teaching Press

Name _____   Date _____

 # Great Globe Locations

North/South	East/West	Location

Catch a Clue

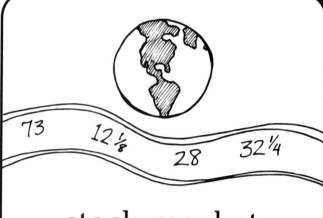

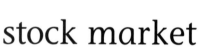

stock market

money

new business idea

grocery store

Our Clues

1 We will be learning about something related to economics—how things are bought and sold.

2 It helps you get things you want.

3 We will not talk about a place of work.

4 It does not "grow on trees"!

Integrating Maps and Money with Reading Instruction © 2002 Creative Teaching Press

Concept Map

Facts we already know about **money and the Great Depression,** and the new facts we have learned

Money and the Great Depression

Word Warm-Up

Which words might you expect to find in a story about **money and the Great Depression?**

loans	economy	farmers
businesses	history	responsible
garbage	savings	unemploy-ment
wages	president	restaurant

Integrating Maps and Money with Reading Instruction © 2002 Creative Teaching Press

Money and the Great Depression

Money makes the world go around. When times are good, people earn enough money to buy the things they need and some things they want. Businesses sell lots of goods to people. They make money. Then, businesses can hire more workers. Throughout history, there have been times that were not good. People did not have jobs. They did not have enough money to buy the things they needed. A very bad time happened many years ago in our country. This time was called the Great Depression.

The Great Depression began in 1929. It was the worst and longest period of unemployment in our history. At one time, one-fourth of the working people did not have jobs. It was also the worst and longest period of slow business growth. Nobody could afford to buy things and businesses failed.

Before 1929, the economy was good. Most people were working. The stock market was very high. Businesses made a lot of money. But not everyone made a lot of money. Farmers did not earn much money for the food they grew. They could not afford to pay for their homes. They lost their farms. The banks that had loaned the farmers money failed when the farms failed. Workers made much less money than businesses earned. Workers could not afford to buy the things businesses made. The stock market was also very high. Many people bought stocks thinking that the prices would go up and they would get rich.

Then, on October 29, 1929, stock prices dropped very fast. This event started the Great Depression. People got scared and sold their stocks at very low prices. They lost a lot of money.

The companies that sold the stocks lost a lot of money. Now their stocks were worth very little. Banks had loaned money to people and companies. Now the people and companies could not repay their loans. This made the banks begin to fail. It got worse when people took their savings out of the banks. People also began to sell the things they owned for any price they could get. They needed the money to buy things just to survive.

Families were really struggling. People lost their homes. Many people had to live in shacks and search garbage cans for food. There were not enough jobs for everyone who wanted to work. Many families moved around the country hoping to find jobs. Those who did have jobs had to accept big pay cuts. People felt lucky if they had any job at all. During the Great Depression, there were very few jobs and many workers. Employers could pay very low wages and people would work anyway. After this time, workers formed labor unions by joining together to demand better working conditions and better pay. If they did not get these things, they refused to work.

When Franklin D. Roosevelt was elected president, people hoped he would do things to end the Great Depression. President Roosevelt created the "New Deal." His plan gave relief for the needy. It also provided jobs. It encouraged business so people could get back to work. It fixed unfair labor practices. It encouraged labor unions to help workers. The New Deal reformed businesses, banks, and the government so a great depression could never happen again.

The goverment began to spend a lot of money on work projects. These projects meant people could have jobs. President Roosevelt hoped that the spending would encourage businesses to start spending, too. It did. As people went back to work, they had more money to spend. Businesses began to make money again. More people got jobs. After many years, the Great Depression began to lift.

Integrating Maps and Money with Reading Instruction © 2002 Creative Teaching Press

Comprehension Questions

Integrating Maps and Money with Reading Instruction © 2002 Creative Teaching Press

Literal Questions

❶ What was the Great Depression? What year did it begin?

❷ What event started the Great Depression?

❸ Name at least three things that happened to people once the Great Depression began.

❹ What is a labor union?

❺ What plan did President Roosevelt create to help end the Great Depression? List at least three ways it helped.

Inferential Questions

❶ Where do you think money comes from?

❷ What do you think the saying "Money makes the world go around" means? Explain your thinking.

❸ The Great Depression began to lift when the country began to spend more money. How do you think this actually helps to bring a nation out of a depression?

❹ What are some ways you think another Great Depression could be avoided?

❺ Why do you think this time in history was named the Great Depression? How do you think families and people were affected emotionally?

Making Connections

❶ Was there ever a time in your life that you wanted or needed something and did not have enough money to buy it? How did you feel? Were you able to get it at a later time? How?

❷ What is the difference between things you need and things you want? List five examples of each. Which are more important? Why?

❸ What are some ways that you can save money and be a responsible spender?

❹ In what ways can you help prevent a mini "Great Depression" from happening in your life?

Sharpen Your Skills

1 Which guide words in the dictionary would help you find the word "monetary"?

- ○ money–monitor
- ○ moist–monarchy
- ○ mischief–mockery
- ○ moment–mongoose

2 What kind of sentence is the following sentence?

How much money did they have to spend?

- ○ exclamatory
- ○ declarative
- ○ interrogative
- ○ command

3 If you wanted to learn more about the Federal Reserve System, which resource would be the most helpful?

- ○ encyclopedia
- ○ dictionary
- ○ thesaurus
- ○ almanac

4 Which part of speech is the word "although" in the following sentence?

Money does not really grow on trees, **although** you may wish it did!

- ○ verb
- ○ noun
- ○ adjective
- ○ conjunction

5 Which word would finish this analogy?

Great Depression is to **lose jobs** like **New Deal** is to _____.

- ○ provide jobs
- ○ failed business
- ○ lose money
- ○ bad times

6 Which word best completes the following sentence?

If you _____ to save your money, then you are showing that you can be responsible with money.

- ○ chose
- ○ choice
- ○ choose
- ○ choosing

Integrating Maps and Money with Reading Instruction © 2002 Creative Teaching Press

Name _____   Date _____

The fourth-grade class at Weaver Elementary is learning about the Great Depression. Four classrooms have each chosen one area to focus on. They will write an economic report to share with the other classes. Use the clues below to decide what topic each class is focusing on.

Clues

❶ Room 27 is not reading and researching about how businesses lost a lot of money because prices dropped very fast.

❷ Neither room 23 nor room 25 is learning about how many people did not have jobs.

❸ The classroom with the lowest room number is learning about a program where workers joined together to demand better working conditions.

❹ The classroom with the second to highest room number is learning about a program the president created to help encourage people to spend money and end the Great Depression.

	Room 21	Room 23	Room 25	Room 27
Labor Union				
New Deal				
Stock Market				
Unemployment Problem				

Room 21 focused on the _____.

Room 23 focused on the _____.

Room 25 focused on the _____.

Room 27 focused on the _____.

Money and the Great Depression

Purpose

The purpose of this activity is for students to experience making economic decisions based on a set income, and then do it again after that income amount changes. Students will relate that experience to what people went through during the Great Depression. Students will also gain an understanding of needs versus wants.

MATERIALS

✔ Family Scenarios reproducible (page 61)
✔ Living Expenses Worksheet (page 62)
✔ scissors
✔ calculators (optional)

Implementation

Make one copy of the Family Scenarios reproducible and eight copies of the Living Expenses Worksheet, and cut apart the scenarios. You will need one scenario and two worksheets for each group of students. Since students will be figuring a lot of numbers, calculators are recommended. It is best to have students complete this activity over two days.

Day 1

Divide the class into four groups. Explain to students that they are going to pretend they are living in the time period just prior to the Great Depression. Give each group one family scenario and one worksheet. Have students read their scenario with their group. Ask students to use the worksheet to decide what things they will buy to live on for one month based on the information in their scenario. Tell students they can purchase more than just the items listed on their scenario if they have extra money, but they cannot exceed their monthly income. Have groups discuss and agree upon the items they will buy and then complete the worksheet. Have a student from each group share with the class the family scenario, the items they chose to buy, and the reasons why they chose these items. Then, discuss as a whole class the differences between the outcome of each group's decisions and why each group came up with different items.

Day 2

Explain to students that the stock market has just crashed! People are losing everything they have—jobs, money, cars. The Great Depression has now begun. Fortunately, each group still has a job. But, unfortunately, their wages have been drastically cut and the prices of goods have remained the same. Now, each group only makes one-quarter of what they previously earned at their job. Give each group another worksheet and the same family scenario. Have each group decide what they will buy based on their new income. Ask groups to agree upon each item, discuss why they think it is important, and then complete the worksheet. Invite a student from each group to share the items they chose and the reasons why they chose these items. Then, discuss as a whole class the differences between the two situations, the differences between the various group situations, and what they learned from the experience.

Integrating Maps and Money with Reading Instruction © 2002 Creative Teaching Press

Family Scenarios

Family #1

○ You are a production worker. You earn $135.00 per month.

○ Your rent and bills cost $12.00 per month.

○ You need to feed five people three meals a day.

○ Your stove just broke and needs to be replaced.

○ Your daughter loves to read at night but cannot see without a light.

○ It is your son's birthday this month. He loves to sled and play with mechanical toys.

○ Your family needs warm clothes for the winter.

Family #2

○ You are an accountant. You earn $320.00 per month.

○ Your rent and bills cost $20.00 per month.

○ Your car payment is $6.00 per month.

○ Your father lives with you and needs an overcoat for winter.

○ You need to feed five people three meals a day.

○ You and your children need some new clothes.

○ It is your wife's birthday this month.

○ You think it is important to put some money in a savings account each week.

Family #3

○ You are a cook. You earn $110.00 per month.

○ Your rent and bills cost $12.00 per month.

○ You need to feed four people three meals a day.

○ You receive three free dinner meals each week from the restaurant you work at.

○ Your family needs some winter clothes.

○ You need a new shirt for work.

○ Your washing machine just broke, and your family needs a new one.

Family #4

○ You are a doctor. You earn $400.00 per month.

○ Your rent and bills cost $30.00 per month.

○ Your car payment is $10.00 per month.

○ You need to feed six people three meals a day.

○ Your family needs warm clothes for the winter.

○ Your wife likes to sew, but she needs a sewing machine.

○ Two of your children's birthdays are in this month. They love to play Ping-Pong™.

○ You think it is important to invest some money in stocks each month.

Names of Group Members:

Living Expenses Worksheet

Your Job: _____ **Amount earned in one month: $** _____

Women's Clothing	Price	Quantity	Cost
Winter Coat	$18.00		
Leather or Suede Bag	$2.25		
Bathrobe	$4.00		
Sweater	$1.00		
Silk Dress	$7.00		
Knitted Rayon Bloomers	$1.00		

Men's Clothing	Price	Quantity	Cost
Broadcloth Shirt	$1.00		
Wool Sweater	$1.00		
Bathrobe	$5.00		
Overcoat	$18.50		
Men's Overalls	$1.50		

Games and Toys	Price	Quantity	Cost
Sled That Steers	$3.95		
Ping-Pong Table	$12.00		
Mechanical Toys	3 for $0.59		
Doll	$1.95		

Items for the Home	Price	Quantity	Cost
Table Lamp	$1.00		
Electric Sewing Machine	$24.00		
Electric Washing Machine	$33.50		
Gas Stove	$19.50		

Meals	Price	Quantity	Cost
Starch, vegetable, and drink	$0.10 per person		
Meat, starch, vegetable, and drink	$0.20 per person		
Meat, starch, vegetable, fruit, and drink	$0.30 per person		
Meat, starch, vegetable, fruit, drink, and dessert	$0.40 per person		

Integrating Maps and Money with Reading Instruction © 2002 Creative Teaching Press

Catch a Clue

What will we learn about in our reading today?

saving money

trading goods and services

opening a bank account

traveling by car

Our Clues

1 It deals with personal economics.

2 You need another person to do this.

3 We will discuss how things are exchanged.

4 Sometimes you do it with your snacks.

Concept Map

Facts we already know about **trading or bartering,** and the new facts we have learned

Trading or Bartering

Integrating Maps and Money with Reading Instruction © 2002 Creative Teaching Press

Word Warm-Up

Which words might you expect to find in a story about **trading or bartering?**

sandwich	exchange	produce
chickens	flowers	value
blacksmith	available	invention
vegetable	auction	haggle

Integrating Maps and Money with Reading Instruction © 2002 Creative Teaching Press

Trading or Bartering

Ryan sat down at the lunch table next to Morgan. He began to take the wrapper off of his sandwich. Then, he noticed Morgan's cupcake. He asked Morgan if she would trade her cupcake for his oatmeal cookies. Morgan told him she would trade if he also gave her half of his sandwich. Ryan thought it sounded like a fair deal, so they traded their food. Both of them felt good about the trade they made.

Ryan and Morgan were practicing the oldest form of trade. People have been doing this since the beginning of civilization. It is called bartering. Bartering is a direct exchange of goods or services. It does not involve any money. In fact, before money was invented, all goods and services were traded using a barter system. Bartering allowed people to make, or produce, only a few things. Then, they could trade their goods or services for others they needed.

A farmer raises chickens. His chickens provide eggs, meat, and feathers. He has more eggs, meat, and feathers than he needs. A woman weaves cloth. She has plenty of cloth to make her own clothes. She does not have much time to grow food. She offers to trade the farmer some cloth in exchange for some eggs. Now the woman can eat and have clothes to wear. Now the farmer has cloth for his clothes in exchange for his extra eggs. Both people have something they need. People can also barter for services. The farmer needs to have his plow repaired. He takes his plow to a blacksmith. He offers the blacksmith some of his vegetables if the blacksmith will repair his plow.

Integrating Maps and Money with Reading Instruction © 2002 Creative Teaching Press

The blacksmith agrees. Now the blacksmith will use his time fixing the plow while the farmer uses his time to grow the vegetables.

The value of a good or service determines what can be traded. The value can be determined in different ways. Some people haggle over the price. They make offers until both people are happy. Some people auction their goods or services. More than one person has to want the good or service. Then, the person who offers the best deal will get the good or service. People might also use set prices. This way the person will only accept a trade if someone offers what he or she wants in exchange.

No matter how people barter, the supply and demand affect the value. The supply is how much of a good or service is available for trade. The demand is how many people want a certain good or service. High supply means the good or service is worth less. Low supply means the good or service is worth more. If there are a lot of potatoes, there are enough for many people to trade. If there are few potatoes, they will be traded to the people who have the most to offer. High demand means higher values. Low demand means lower values.

The problem with bartering is that people have to want the good or service before they will agree to trade. This led to the invention of money. Money allowed people to easily exchange goods and services. It did not matter if a person had something another person wanted. They could exchange goods for money. Then, the money could be used to buy what each person really needed.

Comprehension Questions

Literal Questions

❶ What is bartering?

❷ How did Morgan and Ryan demonstrate the oldest form of trade?

❸ How can the value of a good or service determine what can be traded?

❹ Will a high supply of a good or service mean it is worth more or less? How about a low supply of a good or service?

❺ Why was money invented?

Inferential Questions

❶ Compare and contrast bartering with buying something with money.

❷ What is the difference between goods and services?

❸ If three French bakers are visiting and do not have money to pay for their lunch, what could they do?

❹ What do you think happens to a five-dollar bill after it is used to buy popcorn at the movies? Draw a picture or list the next five places that you think that five-dollar bill will end up.

❺ What is a fair trade?

Making Connections

❶ Do you do more bartering or spending of money? Name three things you have used for bartering and three things you have bought with money.

❷ Which is easier for a child who is your age—bartering or spending money? Explain your thinking.

❸ Pretend you are at a circus. List three things that you would see bartered or sold. Label each item with the form of payment.

❹ Are you saving your money? Why is that important? What are you saving it up to "trade" for?

Integrating Maps and Money with Reading Instruction © 2002 Creative Teaching Press

Sharpen Your Skills

1 Which word best completes the following sentence?

If you want to buy an expensive item, then you have to _____ until you have saved enough money.

- ○ weight
- ○ wate
- ○ waited
- ○ wait

2 Look at these words: careless–useless–senseless.

What is the meaning of the suffix "less"?

- ○ without
- ○ only
- ○ alone
- ○ bad

3 If you wanted to find out in which state the most money was exchanged for goods and services last year, which resource would be the most helpful?

- ○ encyclopedia
- ○ thesaurus
- ○ dictionary
- ○ almanac

4 In the new cafeteria, Shad bought green beans, chicken tacos, and chocolate chip cookies. He exchanged $2.00 for his lunch.

Which of the following words is <u>not</u> an adjective?

- ○ exchanged
- ○ green
- ○ chicken
- ○ chocolate chip

5 Which word would finish this analogy?

Barter is to _____ like **money** is to **cash.**

- ○ shop
- ○ find
- ○ trade
- ○ make

6 Which word best completes the following sentence?

Bartering only works if you have something that someone else is _____ in trading.

- ○ interest
- ○ interested
- ○ interesting
- ○ intersect

Name _____   Date _____

Get Logical

Sandra, Troy, Darren, and Kerrie each have a different type of job. Each of their jobs involves either bartering or selling a good or a service. Use the clues below to decide which good or service each person sells or barters.

Clues

1 Kerrie does not deal with any money transactions, but Darren does.

2 The person who washes cars at a car wash and is paid $10.00 per car is not Troy or Sandra.

3 The person who trades diamonds for sapphires and emeralds with other local jewelers is not Sandra or Troy.

4 The person who exchanges bookkeeping for tutoring with a friend is not a girl.

	Sandra	Troy	Darren	Kerrie
Barters Goods				
Barters Services				
Sells Goods				
Sells Services				

Sandra _____.

Troy _____.

Darren _____.

Kerrie _____.

Integrating Maps and Money with Reading Instruction © 2002 Creative Teaching Press

Bartering Bonanza

Purpose

The purpose of this activity is to bring to life for students the economic concepts of free trade, supply and demand, and bartering and to give them a greater understanding of how bartering works and the pros and cons it involves.

MATERIALS

✔ Bartering Bonanza Announcement (page 72)

✔ items to barter from home

Implementation

Write the date of your Bartering Bonanza on a copy of the Bartering Bonanza Announcement, photocopy a class set of the parent letter, and have each student take it home. Review with students the concepts of bartering, trading, and supply and demand. Explain to students that they will bring in one or two items from home to barter in class in exchange for something else. Encourage students to bring in items that they no longer want that they think someone else might want (e.g., a good book, a game, or art supplies—not their old, stinky socks!). Have students bring in their item a day prior to the Bartering Bonanza. Discuss with students how the "bartering" should take place. Model with a student how to ask for a trade. For example say, *I will trade you my book for your jewelry box.* A student may reply *That does not seem like a fair trade to me, but I will trade you my jewelry box for your book and art supplies.* Discuss rules such as no arguing, lining up in order if there is more than one person wanting to trade for an item, and accepting the answer "no" when it is given or replying respectfully with another trade offer. Ask students to put their items on top of their desk. Invite students to line up single file. Have them walk past each desk to view the items available for trade. Then, let the bartering begin! It is helpful to bring in a few extra items from your home just in case someone forgets to bring something. If all of the items are not traded, ask students if they would like to donate their leftover items to a charity. When the Bartering Bonanza is over, ask students questions such as *How did it feel to barter? Did you want something that you could not have? Was it hard for you to trade your item? Why?*

Bartering Bonanza Announcement

_____
(Date)

Dear Families,

As you know, we have been learning some basic concepts about economics. We have recently learned about bartering and supply and demand. Bartering involves trading items without using any money. Bartering was used to exchange goods and services before money was invented. As I am sure you have seen, students barter all the time. They trade desserts, snacks, sports cards, and magazines.

To further the students' understanding of these concepts, we are going to have a Bartering Bonanza on _____. I am asking each student to bring in one or two items that he or she thinks will be worth trading and no longer needs at home. The item(s) to be bartered should be inexpensive, used, and something that can be given away. Most importantly, the item(s) need to be approved by a guardian first. When you have approved the selected item(s), please fill out the bottom portion of this page and have your child return it to school.

Thank you for helping us put economic principles to work in a fun and memorable way!

Sincerely,

_____

- -

My child, _____ , has my permission to barter his or her _____

_____ for a new item of his or her choice.

_____
(Signature of adult family member)

Integrating Maps and Money with Reading Instruction © 2002 Creative Teaching Press